MUSIC

MUSIC

MERLION ARTS LIBRARY

MUSIC FROM STRINGS

by Josephine Paker

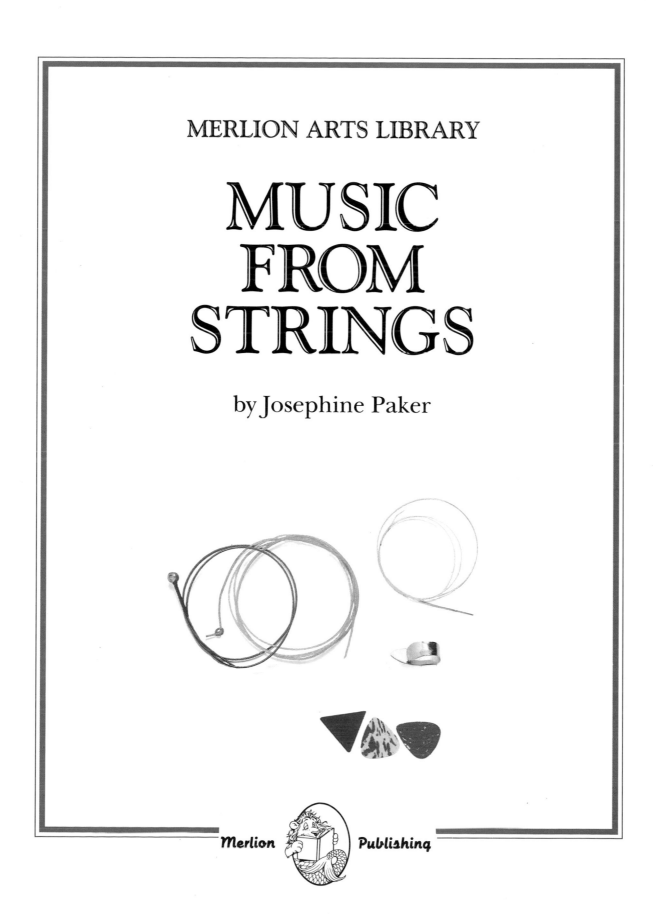

Merlion Publishing

2nd printing 1993

Consultant: Denys Darlow F.R.C.M., F.L.C.M.
Designer: Tracy Carrington

Printed in Great Britain by BPCC Paulton Books

ISBN 1 85737 033 3

Cover photography by Mike Stannard.

Artwork on pages 5, 12, 35 and 36 by Jeremy
Gower; pages 15, 16, 19, 21, 24, 30, 31 and 32
by Kevin Kimber and pages 6, 8—9, 10, 11, 14, 19,
20, 30, 32, 35, 37 and 38 by Andrew Midgley.

Models on pages 5, 6—7, 14 and 28 by Kate Davies.

Photographs on pages 4—5, 6—7, 8, 10, 14, 18,
20—21, 22, 23, 28, 30, 32, 33, 36, 42 and 43 by
Mike Stannard.

CONTENTS

A vibrating string 4

Musical bows 6

Folk fiddles 8

Development of the violin 10

The family of strings 12

The lyre and the harp..14

Lutes with frets..16

Strumming and plucking 18

The guitar..20

Electric guitars 22

Music on the page 24

The sitar of India 26

The world of zithers..28

Playing the keys 30

The versatile piano 32

Playing together in an orchestra....................................34

The human voice 36

Singing in groups..38

Listening to opera 40

What every performer needs 42

Glossary of instruments..44

Index..46

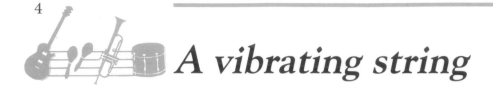

A vibrating string

A Chinese band playing stringed instruments in Beijing Park

You have probably seen instruments which use strings to make a musical sound many times before. But look carefully at the strings on the instruments in the picture above. They're certainly not made from string! Musical strings can be made from metal, plastic, animal gut and even silk. So how do you make a musical noise with a string?

First, you have to fix the string firmly at both ends so that it is stretched tight. If you stretch a rubber band tightly across the top of an empty jar and pull it toward you, or pluck it, you will see how a sound is made. Watch the rubber band shaking very fast just after you pluck it. This movement is called vibration. A vibration sets the air around the rubber band moving in waves which we call sound waves. The waves carry the twanging sound to your ear. You've made a musical sound!

A double bass

A trough zither

High or low

To make sounds into music, the strings on a stringed instrument must be tuned to produce a specific pure sound called a note. You can find out more about notes by turning to pages 24 and 25.

Notes can be high or low. Long or loose strings produce low notes and short or tight strings produce high notes. An instrument's strings are usually stretched and fixed to a particular length so that they always sound the same.

To make a string sound higher or lower, you can shorten it by putting a finger or another kind of stop in the way. You can try this out on a rubber-band harp. All you need is a box to act as a resonator and some rubber bands as strings. Stretch the bands around the box and start plucking. Make different notes by using long and short bands, or by stopping the bands with your fingers.

Resonators

A vibrating string does not make much noise by itself. But if you fix the string across the open part of a hollow container, vibrations from the string will echo around inside it. The vibrations set up sounds which are louder and richer. We call hollow containers that increase the volume of sounds 'resonators' because the sound is echoing, or resonating, inside them. Resonators come in many shapes and sizes. The body of this double bass is an enormous resonator and it makes a low sound, while the narrow trough zither produces a much smaller noise.

Musical bows

According to a Japanese legend, the sun goddess once had an argument with her brother. In a rage, she shut herself in a cave and the whole world was plunged into darkness. So the other gods came up with a plan that would persuade the sun goddess to come out again. They played wonderful melodies on a musical instrument made from six hunters' bows. One of the goddesses started to dance. The gods yelled and clapped their hands. When the sun goddess heard the noise and music, she was curious. She came out of her cave and light returned to the world.

A single string

Stringed instruments which look like hunting bows still exist in Africa and Asia today. They are called musical bows. You can see from the picture below that a musical bow is simply a single string fastened at each end to a flexible stick. The string can be made to move in several ways. You can pluck it with your fingers or tap it with a stick. Or you can use another, smaller bow to make it sound. The two strings rub together and cause each other to vibrate.

Playing a musical bow

Multiple strings

Several single bows can be joined together and attached to a single resonator to make an instrument which creates several sounds at once. We call this instrument a compound musical bow. Each string on each bow is a different length. In this way, each one produces a different note. These compound musical bows are often heard in the music of Central America, Asia and Africa. Look back to the Japanese picture to see a compound musical bow.

Homemade resonators

You can fix any hollow object to a musical bow to help increase the sound it produces. Round vegetables called gourds are often hollowed out, dried, then cut in half to be used as resonators. Half a coconut shell, a tin can or a cooking pot also makes a good resonator. If you hold the bow in your mouth, like the boy in the picture above, you can even use your mouth as the resonator.

Folk fiddles

Folk fiddles are popular stringed instruments used all over Asia, Africa and Europe. Some folk fiddles look very much like musical bows, but some have up to six strings and look more like violins. A folk fiddle is usually played, or bowed, using another bow with horsehair strings.

There are two basic kinds of folk fiddle – a spike fiddle and a short-necked fiddle. The spike fiddle, as you can see from the picture on the right, has a spike at the bottom. It is held upright, with the spike resting on the floor or on the player's knee – if it is not too sharp! A short-necked fiddle is shown in the picture at the top of the next page. It is held horizontally, with the base of the instrument resting against the player's shoulder or chest.

This Turkish spike fiddle is held vertically

Changing pitch

As you know, if you change the length of a string you will change the sound it makes. The note will be higher or lower. This is called changing the pitch of a note. Pressing a finger on the string so that less of it is able to vibrate is one way of changing the pitch. This is easy on most folk fiddles, which have the strings running over a long, thin board called a fingerboard. When you press, or stop, the string with your finger, it presses the string down on the board, shortening it and creating a higher note. Take your finger away – you are back to the full string vibration again. The note you play is lower.

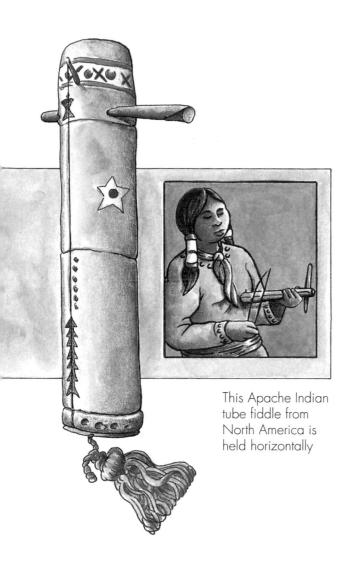

This Apache Indian tube fiddle from North America is held horizontally

Fiddles for dancing

Music from folk fiddles can be bright and lively – just right for dancing! Many fiddlers from European countries such as Hungary play at amazing speed and with great skill. They learn to play the fiddle by ear and can play the most intricate tunes from memory. The most important musician in the Italian picture below is the folk fiddler who stands in the centre. He is playing for a special dance called the tarantella. This was a well-known dance with a fast rhythm which needed quick, exciting music as its accompaniment. Any fiddler who could keep up as the dance went on and on was always in demand!

The pegs and the bridge

On every fiddle there is a mechanism for fixing the exact length and tightness of each string. This means that the string always plays the right note – we say that it is in tune. Can you see the pegs at the head of the fiddle on the left? The strings are fastened to the pegs. By turning the pegs very slightly, you can tighten or loosen the strings to give slightly higher or lower notes.

The strings rest on a raised, curved platform called a bridge. The bridge lifts the strings up and prevents the bow from touching the body of the fiddle so that you play a clear, crisp note.

This painting, by the Italian artist Pietro Fabris, is called *Tarantella with Posillipo in the Background*

Development of the violin

Playing the viol

In the 1500s and 1600s, a concert or small musical gathering would probably echo to the melodies created by a stringed instrument called the viol. This is a six-stringed instrument with a gently sloping bridge which made it easy to play several strings at once. As you can see from the picture on the left, the musician sits down to play the viol, resting the instrument on, or between, the knees. The bow is held with the palm facing outwards and is drawn across the strings to produce a soft, delicate sound. Viols have recently regained their old popularity and groups of viol players, called consorts, are getting together to play this special music.

The violin

The violin is a smaller instrument than the viol, but it makes a louder noise. From about 1700 the violin started to replace the viol in Europe and today it is probably the best known of all western orchestral instruments.

This picture of a violin shows all the parts of the instrument. Can you see the fingerboard, the pegs, the strings and the bridge? The small hollow at the base is called a chin rest. The player positions the chin in the hollow and holds up the violin to play it. The two f-shaped holes are called soundholes. They allow the sound that is resonating inside the body of the violin to escape and give a full, rich note.

A modern violin with bow and resin

The Italian violinist
Niccolò Paganini

Improving the sound

What you cannot see are two important parts inside the body of the violin. One is the soundpost, which is a small stick fixed near the bridge, and the other is the bass bar which runs up between the soundholes. These two parts make sure that the vibrations spread throughout the whole body of the instrument.

The bow

The violin bow is a flexible stick with thin strands of horsehair stretched from one end to another. The hair can be tightened by turning a small nut fixed to one end. The hair needs to be coated with a soft, sticky gum called resin to make the string vibrate properly.

The best in the world?

The Italian musician Antonio Stradivari was a great violin maker. The instruments he made are now about 300 years old but they still make a wonderful

sound. Those that still exist are highly prized and sell for a great deal of money. We still don't know the secret of Stradivari's success – it was probably a combination of the design, the thickness of the wood and the varnish.

In the 1800s, the Italian violinist Niccolò Paganini revolutionized the technique of violin playing. You can see him playing a violin in the picture. He introduced new, exciting methods of fingering and bowing. He often made up the music as he went along and sometimes used tricks such as putting on a blindfold, or cutting one or two of the strings of his violin and continuing to play on the other two strings. People thought he was insane, but he certainly made an amazing sound!

Some of the most talented modern musicians are violinists. The British violinist Yehudi Menuhin started learning the violin when he was four and was already a brilliant player by the age of seven. He founded a school in England for musically talented children. This picture shows the famous Korean violinist Kyung Wah Chung.

The Korean violinist
Kyung Wah Chung

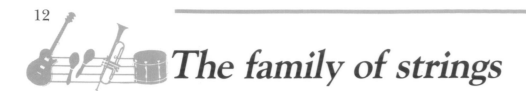

The family of strings

A string quintet

The violin may be an important stringed instrument, but it is only one of a family of instruments. The other members are the viola, the cello and the double bass.

1. violin
2. viola
3. cello
4. double bass

1   2   3   4

These four instruments make a similar sound, each at a different pitch. We call the four pitches treble, alto, tenor and bass. The violin plays the highest pitch – the treble. The viola plays the alto, the cello the tenor and the double bass provides the low bass notes. So when they are played together in a group, the effect is very pleasant.

There is a lot of music written especially for the four instruments of a string quartet. A string quartet consists of two violins, a viola and a cello.

Look at the picture on the left. You can see the five instruments that form the slightly larger string quintet. Can you identify the instruments the musicians are playing?

The viola

The viola is just like the violin, but it is slightly larger, so the sound it makes is lower. The mellow sound of the viola is important to the string quartet. It plays the middle notes of the musical picture.

The cello

The cello, whose proper name is the violoncello, produces a wonderful rich sound. It can cover a wider range of notes than any of the other members of the string family. Its large body provides good resonance and its notes are broad and mellow. This makes the cello an ideal instrument to listen to on its own when it is not providing the tenor theme.

The cello is far too big to play under your chin! You sit down with the instrument between your legs and the neck rests on your shoulder. A spike on the base of the cello rests on the floor.

Double bass

The double bass is the largest string instrument. It is about 2 metres tall, and its strings are 108 centimetres long. Travelling around with a double bass is not easy! Some players find it most comfortable to sit on the edge of a high stool when they play. Others, like the famous American jazz musician Charlie Mingus, prefer to stand up. You can see Charlie Mingus playing in the picture on the right.

The American jazz musician Charlie Mingus

The lyre and the harp

There is a legend from Ancient Greece about a man called Orpheus, the son of the Greek god Apollo. Orpheus played an instrument called a lyre.

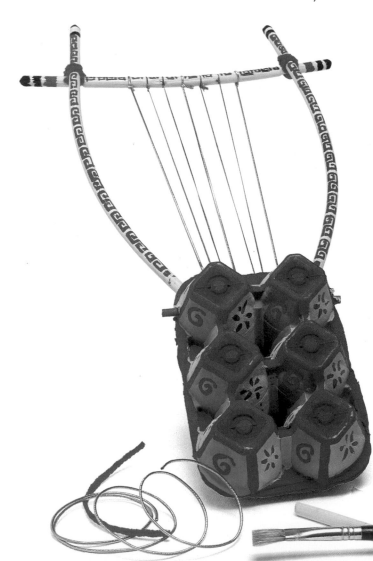

He played it so beautifully that he charmed all the animals with his music.

One day Orpheus's wife Eurydice was bitten by a snake and died. She was taken down into the underworld. In despair, Orpheus took his lyre and went in search of her. On entering the underworld, he was brought before its queen, Persephone. He begged the queen to release his wife and so charmed her with his music that she agreed, on one condition. Orpheus must not turn to look at his wife as he led her back to the outside world. But Orpheus was impatient. Just as he was leaving the underworld he turned round. Instantly Eurydice vanished. Soon after, Orpheus died of grief.

What is a lyre?

The lyre that is mentioned in this sad story is an instrument with strings that stretch between a resonator to a frame called a crossbar. The player plucks the strings with bare fingers. Orpheus's lyre may have looked something like this model. Its resonator was probably an empty tortoiseshell.

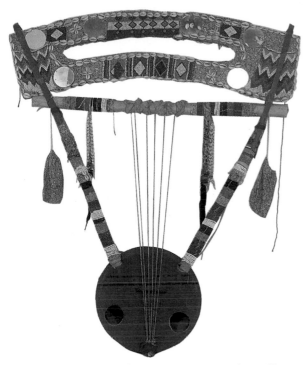

This magnificent lyre is called a bowl lyre. It comes from Ethiopia

The folk harp in the picture below comes from Peru. It has 28 strings. Each string is tuned to a particular note. If you run your finger across all the strings, you can play a pattern of notes which follow on from each other, called a scale. This is just like the scale you play when you run your finger over the white notes on a piano. Can you see the holes in the harp's resonator? These allow the resonating sound to escape.

A Peruvian harp player

In ancient times, lyres were popular all over the world. Today they are played mainly in parts of Africa, where they often accompany singing in religious festivals. The highly decorated lyre in the picture above comes from Ethiopia.

The lyre   The harp

Large and small harps

Harps are also made from strings attached to a frame. But harps are different from lyres in one important way. Look at the diagram above. You can see that the strings of the folk harp are set at an angle so that they run from the resonator to the instrument's neck. The lyre's strings run straight from the resonator to the crossbar. Harps are usually much larger than lyres.

Lutes with frets

If you were learning to play the violin, how would you know where to place your fingers to play the notes you want? Your teacher would need to show you where to press down on the fingerboard. Then, of course, you would have to practise and practise until you knew all the positions by heart and could play quickly and well.

On the fingerboard of some instruments, such as lutes and guitars, you will find ridges called frets. Frets are fixed across the fingerboard at certain intervals to help you to play the right note. When you press a string above a particular fret, the string vibrates only between the fret and the bridge on the resonator. Each fret marks a different note that a single string can play. When a string is pressed in this way, it is called 'stopping the string'. Frets mean you can learn where to place your fingers more easily.

1. Stopping a string without frets
2. Using frets to stop a string

1

2

This picture, by the Italian artist Michelangelo Merisi da Caravaggio, is called *Young Man Playing a Lute*

A Portuguese
fish lute

The lute family

Lutes are stringed instruments which are popular all over the world. They usually have frets to help the player produce a wide range of notes. The soft sound of a lute makes it the perfect instrument for accompanying songs.

Lutes come in many different shapes and sizes. The folk lute from China shown in the picture above is called a ch'in. It is also known as the moon guitar, because it has such a round body – just like a full moon. Many moon guitars are decorated in bright colours like this one.

The amazing Portuguese lute in the picture on the right has a body carved in the shape of a fish. This is the resonator. Can you see its sharp teeth and the detailed carved scales?

Strumming and plucking

A banjo

A ukulele

An American painting of a banjo player from the early 1800s

During the 1700s and 1800s, many thousands of Africans were brought to America to work as slaves. Many worked on the tobacco and cotton plantations in the southern states. In the picture at the bottom of the page you can see plantation workers dancing to the music of a banjo. The banjo is a stringed instrument which developed from long-necked lutes that were brought to America from Africa.

A banjo has between four and nine metal strings. Its body is round, with a skin or parchment stretched over it somewhat like a drum. A metal frame keeps the parchment firmly in place. The back of the banjo is often left open, so the noise it makes is not very resonant. Both banjos and ukuleles make a light, twangy sound when the strings are plucked with the fingertips.

Strum away

This large picture shows the British entertainer George Formby playing a ukulele. The ukulele comes from Hawaii and looks like a small guitar. You can see from the picture that it has four strings. Its name comes from a Hawaiian word meaning flea – because the ukulele is much smaller than a real guitar!

The strings are plucked with the fingers of one hand while the fingers of the other hand press the strings down on the fingerboard to make the different notes. Banjos and ukuleles can also be played in a different way by running the fingers over all the strings together. This makes a smoother sound and is known as strumming. You do not have to be able to read music to play instruments like the ukulele or the banjo. You just read a chart which tells you where to put your fingers.

Some people use a plectrum to pick the strings. This creates a different sound. They either hold the plectrum or fix it to their fingers, as you can see in the diagram below. You can read more about plectra on page 21.

Using a plectrum

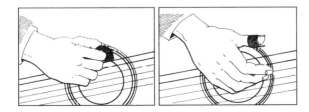

The British ukulele player George Formby

The guitar

A Spanish guitar

When you think of the classical, or acoustic, guitar, you probably think of Spain and flamenco dancers stamping their feet to the exciting rhythm of a guitar. During the 1800s you would have heard a guitar being played in every village in Spain. It was the time when the guitar reached the peak of its popularity. Each of these guitars was based on a design by a Spanish instrument maker called Antonio Torres. In fact, all six-stringed, classical guitars, like the one in the picture above, are based upon Torres's original design. They have a wooden body which acts as a resonator, and a round soundhole to let out the musical sound.

Segovia

One of the most famous classical guitarists of all time was also a Spaniard. His name was Andrés Segovia. When Segovia was a boy, his parents did not approve of him playing the guitar. He had to practise in secret, without a teacher. He watched flamenco players and practised and studied, and practised some more. Eventually, all of Segovia's hard work paid off. His first concert, in Granada in 1909, was a great success and marked the beginning of Segovia's career as a brilliant guitarist.

The Spanish classical guitarist Andrés Segovia

Folk guitars

Guitars designed to play folk music are usually slightly different from the classical, Spanish guitar. Classical guitars usually have strings made of animal gut or nylon, while folk guitars usually have steel strings. Folk guitars also tend to have a narrower fingerboard. Folk players like the Gypsy Kings, a lively band from South America, hold the guitars high up across their bodies as they play fast Spanish rhythms.

A member of the Gypsy Kings folk group

The bottleneck

Folk musicians often need to hold down all the guitar strings as they strum. This can be difficult! To help them do this, they use a metal tube called a bottleneck, which you can see in the picture below.

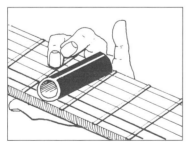

Using a bottleneck

The bottleneck is worn on a finger and touches several strings at once. The musician moves the bottleneck up and down the strings to produce an effective sliding sound.

Plectra

Many guitar players use a plectrum to pluck the strings. This protects their fingers as they play. Plectra come in different shapes and sizes. The most common kind has a pointed end to pluck the strings and a rounded end to hold. Some plectra are shaped to fit over the finger or thumb so that they can be worn rather than gripped. There are several different kinds of plectra in the picture below. As you can see, plectra can be made from metal or plastic.

Different kinds of plectra

Electric guitars

An electric guitar and amplifier

The electric guitar has the same name as the classical guitar, but it is a quite different instrument. You can see from the picture on the left that the electric guitar has a solid body. The vibrations of the strings are changed into electric signals. The signals are sent to a machine called an amplifier, which turn them back into sound. A loudspeaker then picks up the sound and increases it even further. The amplifier and loudspeaker are often housed in the same box, as they are in the picture. The result is a sound that is not at all like a Spanish guitar!

If you go to a music shop and look at the names of some of the electric guitars for sale, you will probably see a brand called Gibson. Orville Gibson was an American musician who developed the first electric guitars. Other kinds of electric guitars are also named after the people who developed them – Les Paul and Leo Fender are two other well-known names.

Special effects

A player can make an electric guitar sound different by using one of the special effects of an amplifier. If a wobbly note is required, the player presses a pedal known as a vibrator. A fuzz-box produces a whirring sound. A reverb makes an echo like the one you get when you sing in the shower. The wah-wah pedal does just what you would expect – it makes the sound come and go with a wailing wah-wah noise!

Playing the electric guitar

Playing the electric guitar is a skill which depends very much on the player's own personality. Most players are self-taught and many prefer to be able to make up, or improvise, the music they play instead of playing something a composer has already written down.

Rock and roll

In the 1950s, rock and roll exploded onto the musical scene. Rock and roll music is a mixture of folk, jazz and rhythm and blues and the electric guitar is an important instrument in this music. The bass electric guitar was developed to provide the low notes in a rock and roll group. It usually has only four strings, which are thicker and longer than the strings on an ordinary guitar. Sometimes bass guitars don't have frets.

Great players like the American guitarist Jimi Hendrix showed the world that the electric guitar could be made into as personal an instrument as the human voice. Look at Jimi Hendrix's expression in this picture. He is completely involved in his music!

The American electric guitarist Jimi Hendrix

An electric bass guitar

Music on the page

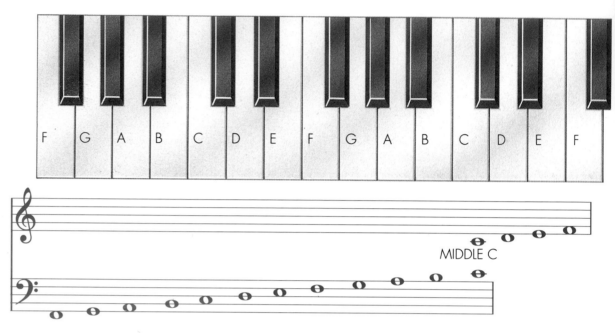

MIDDLE C

Composers write down their music. That way they can be sure that it will be performed just as they want it to be. Writing and reading music is like writing and reading words. But to write or read music you have to learn another language.

The language of music

Notes are like words – they make up the language of music. Musical notes are named after the first seven letters of the alphabet. The C nearest the middle of a keyboard is called middle C. Music is written on sets of five lines, each called staves. A stave is like a ladder. The higher up the ladder you are, the higher the note sounds.

At the beginning of each stave there is a sign called a clef. The treble clef 𝄞 shows that the notes are above middle C and the bass clef 𝄢 shows that the notes are below middle C.

The picture above shows you how the notes on a keyboard are written down on the staves. You can find out more about keyboards on pages 30–33.

Lengths of notes

Look at a metre rule. You'll see that it can be divided into 100 centimetres. And you know that a centimetre can be divided into 10 millimetres. Lengths of musical notes are measured in a similar way. Long notes can be divided up into shorter notes.

Let's start with a long note called a whole note (also called a semibreve). It is written like this 𝅝

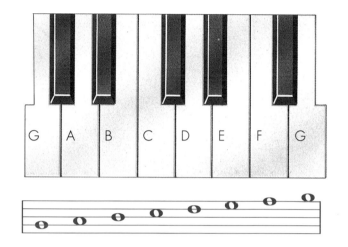

Every whole note is worth two half notes (or minims) 𝅗𝅥

Every half note is worth two quarter notes (or crotchets) ♩

Every quarter note is worth two eighth notes (or quavers) ♪

Music usually has regular groups of beats. When music is written down, it is written in sections called bars or measures.

Chords

When you want several notes to be played together, you write down all the notes and layer them one on top of the other. This layer is called a chord. A chord looks like this:

Scales

Music is usually based on a series of notes called a scale. You can use scales made up of different notes. Musical pieces from other parts of the world may sound strange to you because they are based on scales which are different from the one you are used to hearing.

Western music is usually based on a scale of eight notes. This scale goes from one note to the same note eight notes, or an octave, higher. For example, the scale of C goes C, D, E, F, G, A, B, C:

Chinese, Japanese, and most other eastern music is based on a 5-note scale called the pentatonic scale. It looks like this:

Eastern music is generally much freer and more individual than western music. People are encouraged to compose and improvise the music as they go along. Some Indian music uses notes that lie between the notes which are written in western music. Indian music is not usually written down. The musicians learn to play an instrument by ear, by copying and listening to great players. You can read more about this on the next page.

The sitar of India

An old Indian print of a sitar player

The sitar is the most popular instrument in northern India. If you look at the picture of the sitar you will see that it has a complicated arrangement of strings. Six or seven main strings are played with a wire plectrum. The strings run over frets, which are like metal hoops. You can move the frets to different positions. Under the main strings there are between 9 and 13 other strings, called sympathetic strings. These strings vibrate when the main strings are played.

You might also hear another background noise which is lower than the sympathetic strings. This is the sound of the drone strings, which make a continuous low tone below the main melody. When you listen to the sitar, you might think that there were two or three instruments playing together. Of course, this complicated arrangement of strings means that the sitar is a difficult instrument to play. Many new players learn from skilled sitar players.

This diagram shows you how the strings of a sitar are arranged

Ragas

Traditional Indian music is not written down. Performers learn groups of notes called ragas and develop their own way of playing them. They improvise the music as they go along. A raga is a combination of a scale and a melody. Each raga has its own mood, such as happiness, sorrow or peace. The different ragas are meant to be played at different times of the day or year. Musicians choose the raga very carefully, often not announcing until the last moment which one they intend to play.

A sitar

A special sound

The Indian musician Ravi Shankar is one of the best-known sitar players in the world. Look at the picture below. Can you see how hard Ravi Shankar concentrates as he plays? His music swoops and slides to the accompaniment of special drums called tablas. Audiences all over the world have been amazed by his playing.

Ravi Shankar has performed to enthusiastic listeners in western countries. The violinist Yehudi Menuhin and the pop group The Beatles have both performed with him, making an interesting mix of the music of east and west.

The Indian sitar player Ravi Shankar

The world of zithers

Many instruments are made up of part of one instrument and part of another. The zither is an instrument which is partly a harp and partly a lute. It has several strings which stretch from one end of the instrument to the other. Some zithers are plucked like harps, while others are stopped with the fingers and plucked, like the strings of a lute.

The simplest zithers are made from a hollowed-out piece of wood. A length of string is laced backwards and forwards across the zither and supported by wooden sticks as bridges at either end. This kind of zither is called a tube zither.

Many tube zithers have a slit cut into the top which acts as a soundhole. This means that the twanging strings sound more resonant. Tube zithers are most common in Africa, where they are played as accompanying instruments.

Make your own tube zither

You could make a simple tube zither from an old plastic bottle. Ask an adult to help you cut a wide slit lengthwise along one side of the bottle. Tie some string tightly around each end of the cylinder. Cut some pieces of string and thread a bead onto each one. Now tie the strings onto the string at each end of the bottle. Paint the bottle in bright colours or decorate it with cut-out pictures to give it a more authentic look.

Now try playing your zither. You may need to tighten your strings to get an effective sound. You can also use stretched rubber bands as your strings. How does this change the sound?

Long zithers

In China and Japan, you often see zithers which are so long that they need to be rested on the floor or on a low table to be played. The koto, from Korea, has 13 strings made of silk. The strings rest on high bridges which are movable. The player alters the pitch of

the note by moving the bridges backwards and forwards. In the picture you can see the player's right hand plucking the strings and the left hand pressing the strings against the bridges to create notes of different pitch.

time after they are hit, so the sounds become blurred. Can you see a dulcimer being played in the Tibetan village orchestra in the picture below?

A South Korean kolo player

The dulcimer

The dulcimer is a kind of zither which is often used to play folk music in the countries of eastern Europe but they are found all over the world. The strings can be plucked or, more usually, hit with small wooden hammers. Sometimes the heads of these hammers are double-sided, with one side made of soft leather and the other of hard leather. This means that soft and loud sounds can be produced. The strings vibrate for a long

A Tibetan village orchestra

Playing the keys

A keyboard

Did you know that a keyboard instrument like the piano is actually a stringed instrument? If you open the lid of a piano and look inside, you will see the strings. There are three kinds of stringed keyboard instruments. They are the clavichord, the harpsichord and the piano. All three use a different way of sounding the strings. The oldest of the group is the clavichord, which dates back to about 1400. The clavichord makes a very soft musical sound.

Playing a
clavichord

Inside a clavichord

This diagram shows how the clavichord strings are played. When you press down one of the keys on the keyboard, a piece of metal called a tangent shoots up and hits a pair of strings. This makes the strings vibrate. The tangent stays in contact with the strings until you take your finger off the key. It drops back into position and the note finishes when the string stops vibrating.

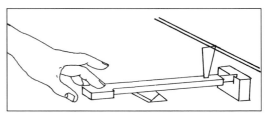

A tangent
hits a clavichord
string to make
it vibrate

The clavichord is a small instrument. Some clavichords do not have legs and are rested on a table to be played. The quietness of clavichord music means that it is better suited to personal performances in a small room than to a performance in a large concert hall. Clavichords are being made again today and are popular among people who like to play old music on the right kind of instrument.

The harpsichord

The picture on the right is a harpsichord. You can see that it looks like a grand piano, although it doesn't sound like one. It has a bright, twangy tone. Look at the diagram below to see how a harpsichord's strings are sounded. They are plucked, not hit. When you press down on a harpsichord key, a plectrum made of a strip of plastic or leather jumps up and plucks the string, making it sound. The note dies away as soon as the key is released. The harpsichord makes a clear, crisp musical sound, which can be very powerful.

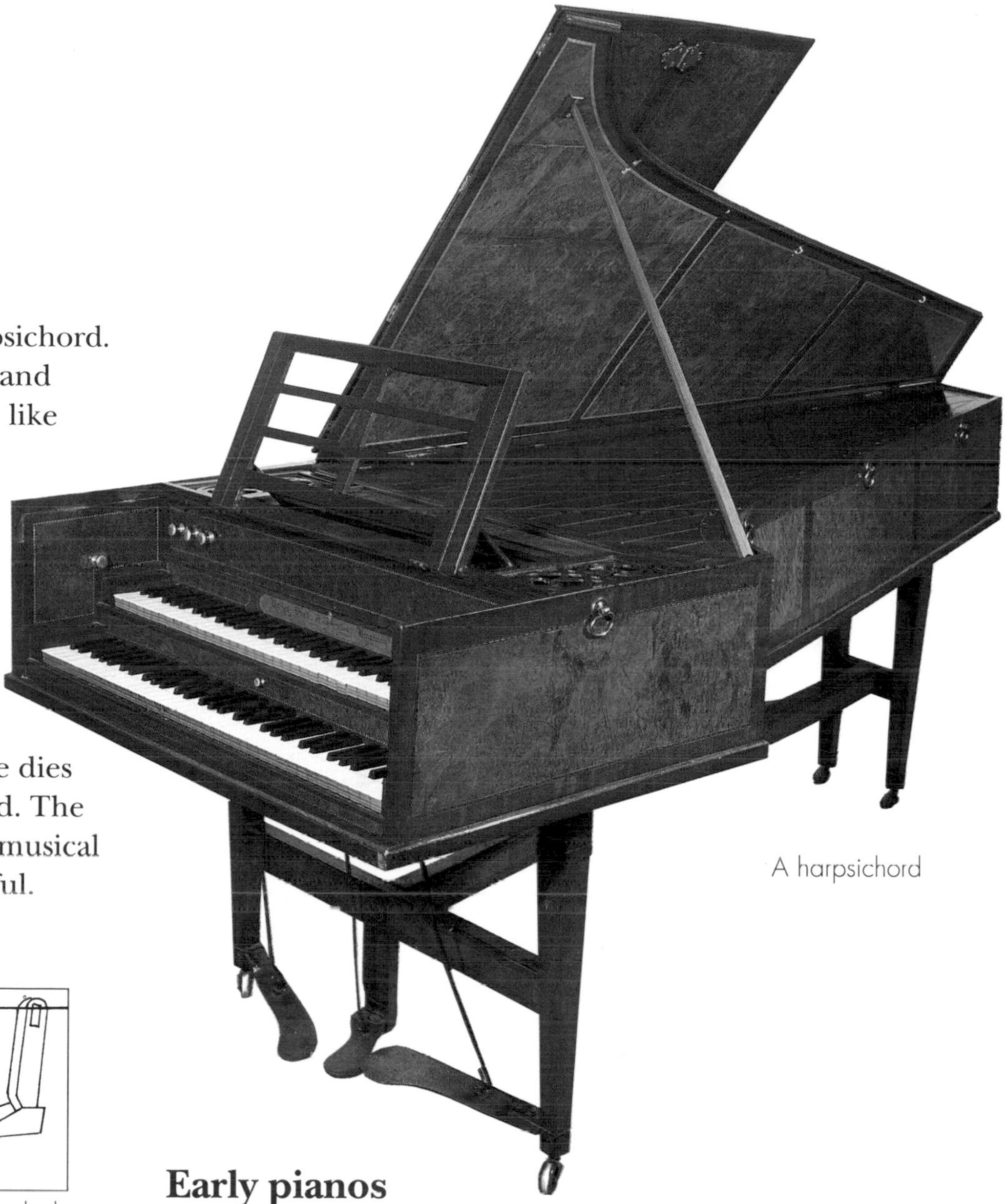

A harpsichord

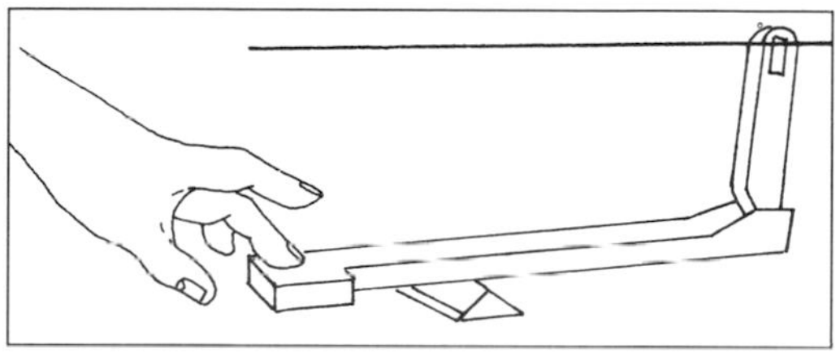

A plectrum plucks a harpsichord string to make it sound

Some harpsichords have two keyboards, or manuals. They also have pedals and controls, called stops, which help the player to create different sounds – loud or soft. The harpsichord was a very popular instrument between about 1600 and 1800. Today, it is used mainly to perform music written during that period by composers such as the famous German composer Johann Sebastian Bach.

Early pianos

The first piano was made in the early 1700s by the Italian Bartolomeo Cristofori. He designed his instrument so that the strings were struck by a padded hammer which immediately fell away from the string. This happened whether or not the player had released the key. As a result, the player could directly affect the sound the instrument made by the way he or she touched the keys. A gentle touch made a gentle noise, a drumming touch made a striking noise and smooth playing helped to join the notes together.

The versatile piano

The musician crouches over his piano keyboard, his long hair flops over his face, while his fingers thunder over the keys at an incredible speed. The caricature above shows the Hungarian pianist Franz Liszt who lived in the 1800s. His performances amazed his audiences because he played incredibly difficult sequences and hardly ever made a mistake. But Liszt was not only a brilliant pianist, he was also a composer.

A caricature of the Hungarian composer and pianist Franz Liszt

Strengthening the instrument

In the time of Liszt, pianos were not as strongly built as they are today. So after only a short burst of Liszt's ferocious playing, the piano sometimes fell to pieces!

Piano makers have improved the instrument a great deal over the years. A modern piano has an iron frame with steel strings stretched over it. The strings are stretched at very high tension, so the frame needs to be very strong. High notes have three strings each, middle notes two and low bass notes have just one thick string. Behind the strings is a soundboard, which resonates when the strings vibrate.

The inside story

The diagram below shows you what happens inside the piano when you press down on a key on the keyboard. First, a hammer strikes the strings, making them vibrate. If they went on vibrating after you went on to play other notes, the sound would become blurred. To prevent this, each note has a damper. A damper is a small pad which falls sharply against the strings when you let go of the key and stops the strings from vibrating.

A hammer strikes the piano string to make it vibrate

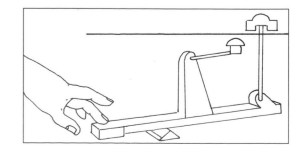

Music for pianos

The piano provides a wide range of notes and many composers have written wonderful music for it. Composers of the 1700s, such as the Austrian Wolfgang Amadeus Mozart, wrote splendid music for the piano. But pianos in Mozart's time had a quieter, drier tone than we are now used to hearing and many people think that Mozart's music sounds best when it is played on an old instrument. Have you ever played the piano? If you have, you probably know that pianos come in different sizes.

A grand piano

Grand piano

You can play on an upright piano which fits into a small room, or you might be lucky enough to play on a concert grand piano, like the one in the picture. It is 3 metres long and takes up a lot more space. You really need a concert hall to play a grand piano in! However, whatever size you play, the piano has to be the greatest of all solo instruments!

Playing together in an orchestra

Have you ever been to a concert where the music is played by an orchestra? If so, you'll have sat eagerly waiting while the players came onto the stage, carrying their instruments. The violinists tighten their bows and make sure their chin rests are comfortable. The cellists adjust their spikes. The oboe player plays an A note. All the other players tune their instruments to match the oboe's A. Finally, when all is ready, the conductor comes on stage and raises the white stick, or baton. There is silence.

The baton comes down and the orchestra starts to play. The concert has begun!

The conductor's job

A large orchestra can have as many as 100 musicians playing together. No wonder it makes an impressive noise! To keep the performance under control, the orchestra needs a conductor. The conductor keeps the players in time and guides the mood of the music.

The BBC Symphony Orchestra, London

He uses movements of his baton and facial expressions to tell the musicians when to play quietly, when to play loudly, when to start and stop or when to slow down or draw the music out. Try conducting some taped music using a small stick or ruler as a baton.

Behind the scenes

When you see an orchestra playing, you may think the conductor's job is an easy one. It may look as if all that is required is to stand there and beat time! But behind all this are long hours of practice time, called rehearsals, which the conductor has put in with the players. The conductor tells the orchestra how the music is to be interpreted. What do you think would happen if the conductor left the orchestra to play by itself? The sound could soon become disorganized.

Every conductor has a strong idea about how a piece of music should sound. If you can, try to compare two recordings of the same music with different conductors. You might hear some interesting differences!

1. play quietly
2. play loudly
3. come in
4. play expressively
5. stop playing

This drawng shows where the musicians in an orchestra sit

The human voice

Take a deep breath. Now sing any note you like, letting the air out slowly. Can you feel your throat vibrating as the air comes out? It may seem unlikely, but your voice is a stringed instrument. It has its own vibrating strings and resonator in just the same way as a stringed instrument like a guitar does.

Your strings are the vocal cords in your voicebox, or larynx. Vocal cords are ribbons of skin which stretch across the larynx – you can see them in the picture below. When you sing or talk, air is forced across the cords, making them vibrate. You can see for yourself how your larynx works. If you blow up a balloon and stretch the neck to make a narrow slit, you'll hear a screeching noise as the air rushes out. That's just what happens in your larynx, only your voice sounds better than the balloon!

Now try humming through your nose. Can you feel your nose buzzing? That's because your nose is one of your voice's resonators. The vibrations also resonate in your head, mouth, throat and chest.

High and low

You sing high notes by tightening your vocal cords. As you come down the scale, the cords become looser. Everyone has his or her own comfortable range. The highest singing voice is the soprano. In a child, this is known as treble. Then comes the alto (called counter tenor in a man). Men usually sing in one of two ranges – either tenor or bass.

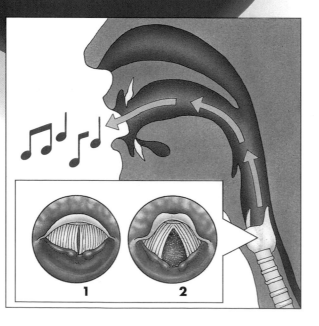

The vocal cords move to produce different sounds:

1. close together to make high sounds
2. far apart to make low sounds

The famous Italian opera singer Luciano Pavarotti

Ways of using your voice

There are many different styles of singing. You can probably think of several. You may have heard a folk singer crooning softly or the clear tones of a choirboy. Maybe you have heard an Islamic preacher, or muezzin, calling people to prayer in a mosque or an Austrian's yodelling call echoing back from a mountainside. Pop and rock singers use microphones to make their voices sound louder, so they can sing quite softly and still be heard by a large audience. You can use your personal stringed instrument to sing whenever you feel like it!

A microphone

Singing in groups

A choir

The music of a group of singers, called a choir, was an important part of church services in medieval Europe. Monks in monasteries used to sing all of the services in Latin. Today, you might hear music sung by choirs which is based on this church tradition. It is called choral music.

Singing a story

Many people enjoy taking part in large-scale musical performances called oratorios. Oratorios are based on Bible stories from the Jewish and Christian religions, but they do not have to be performed in church.

Oratorios are performed by an orchestra, a choir and soloists, who sing important parts on their own. A special singer called a narrator tells the story in song. The German composer Johann Sebastian Bach is well known for his church cantatas. A cantata is a story sung by one or two singers who are accompanied by various instruments.

The German composer Johann Sebastian Bach

Gospel music

Gospel music is a kind of church singing which combines elements of hymns, jazz and black American religious folksongs. Gospel choirs like the one in the picture below sing with great warmth and emotion. A gospel concert always involves the audience, who end up stamping, clapping their hands and dancing. It's great fun!

Other groups

Not all singing groups are choirs, of course. You can probably think of many other kinds of singing musical groups. There are pop and rock bands, folk singers, jazz bands and many more. All these groups use the distinctive sound of voices singing together.

Popular music

Most pop groups use their voices as well as their instruments to make music. You probably know all the words of many pop songs which are popular today. You'll know that some of these pop groups are only popular for a short time. A new group takes their place and they are soon forgotten.

But there are exceptions. The British group called The Beatles wrote and performed songs in the 1960s and 1970s that seem likely to remain popular for a long time to come. Perhaps you have a favourite pop group at the moment. Do you think their songs will still be popular in 350 years' time? That's how long ago Bach wrote his choral music!

An American gospel choir

Listening to opera

The Italian opera
singer Lucia Popp

What IS she singing about? She is making a lovely sound, but you can't understand the words! These thoughts might cross your mind if you were listening to a musical play called an opera. The German composer Richard Wagner wrote what he called music-dramas. He wrote both words and music. Built into the music were themes that represented characters or ideas in the story. So unless you do your homework on a Wagner opera, you might find it difficult to understand.

Early opera

In early opera, the performers told a story by singing it, instead of speaking it. This kind of singing is called recitative. A few years later, the Italian composer Claudio Monteverdi made opera more lively by adding choruses and dances to the recitative.

During the 1600s, opera became very popular and composers wrote more and more of them to satisfy public demand. The stories were often quite fantastic and the operas were often specially designed

A scene from the opera *Turandot*

to show off the voice of a famous singer. But in the 1700s, the Austrian composer Wolfgang Amadeus Mozart wrote both serious operas that were entertaining and comic operas that were well written. The standard of opera rose to new heights.

Grand opera

The grand opera of the 1800s is what many people today think of as true opera. It has colourful costumes, romantic music and extravagant acting. These operas are still popular today, with lavish performances like this scene from *Turandot*, an opera by the Italian composer Giacomo Puccini. The great modern opera singers, like the New Zealand opera star Kiri Te Kanawa, draw huge audiences to each performance.

So, even if you do have difficulty following the words of an opera, you can still enjoy the drama of the performance. Or perhaps you would prefer to see a musical? This is a modern

form of opera, somewhere between classical or grand opera and an evening of popular music, which also offers dancing and catchy tunes.

A programme from a modern musical

COLE PORTER'S CAN-CAN

What every performer needs

Every performer needs a few simple pieces of equipment, if nothing else, to give a successful performance. It is well worth spending a little time beforehand to make sure of a worthwhile result.

A metronome

The metronome

First make sure you play your music at the right speed. A machine called a metronome tells you what the speed should be. But how fast is fast? How slow is slow? It's not always easy to decide how quickly a piece should be played. Composers often give an indication of the speed by putting numbers at the beginning of a piece of music. These numbers show how many beats there should be in a minute, from a slow 40 to a whizzing 208. The metronome helps you know exactly how quickly to play. You set the metronome by positioning a weight against the marks on a bar until it points to the chosen speed. Then you set it ticking, like a clock. Each tick represents one beat.

The tuning fork

When you play an instrument, especially in a group, you have to make sure that every instrument plays each note at the same pitch. The pitch must not vary from instrument to instrument, or the music will be out of tune.

Sound is caused by vibrations of air. Scientists measure pitch by counting how many vibrations a sound makes in one second. Low notes have few, slow vibrations, and high notes have many, fast ones.

The note A, which many instruments use to tune from, is fixed at 440 vibrations per second. This is known as concert pitch. Instruments tuned to concert pitch will sound the same all over the world. You can get the correct pitch of a note from a device called a tuning fork. This is a piece of metal that sounds a precise note when it is struck gently on a surface. You may also have seen an electrical tuner like the one in the picture. This picks up the sound waves from the note you play and shows them on a screen.

Once you've fixed the pitch of one note, you can match the pitch of all the others to it. Now you can put your music on a music stand and the performance can begin. Good luck!

An electrical tuner

A tuning fork

GLOSSARY OF INSTRUMENTS

banjo: A stringed instrument with a long neck and round body consisting of a parchment skin stretched over a metal hoop.

cello: The bass member of the violin family. It is a large instrument, played resting on the floor with the neck against the player's shoulder.

clavichord: A small keyboard instrument popular in the 1400s and 1500s.

double bass: The largest member of the violin family, it plays the lowest notes. Usually 2 metres high.

dulcimer: An eastern instrument similar to the zither. It is a shallow box over which wire strings are strung. The strings are hit with small wooden hammers.

electric guitar: Similar to the guitar, but the body is not hollow. Vibrations from the strings are changed into electrical waves which pass to an amplifier and onto a loudspeaker.

folk fiddle: This is a stringed instrument which is played with a bow. Short-necked fiddles and spike fiddles are two kinds of fiddles.

guitar: The classical or Spanish guitar is a well-known six-stringed instrument played all over the world.

harp: A series of strings stretched from a resonator across a frame. The strings are plucked.

harpsichord: A keyboard instrument, similar to the piano, but much older. When the player presses a key, a device plucks the string inside the instrument.

lute: A stringed instrument played all over the world. The fingerboard of a lute has frets to make stopping a string easier.

lyre: An ancient stringed instrument with strings stretching between a resonator to a frame called a crossbar. The strings are plucked.

musical bow: An instrument which looks like a hunting bow. It has a single string which is plucked. Several musical bows can be put together to form a multiple string bow.

piano: The most popular of the keyboard instruments. Pianos can produce a range of loud and soft notes.

sitar: A stringed instrument from India. It has main strings, sympathetic strings and drone strings.

ukulele: A small guitar which originally came from Hawaii.

viol: A six-stringed instrument which is played resting between the player's knees. It was popular in the 1500s and 1600s.

viola: Slightly larger than the violin, the viola has four strings and plays the middle notes of a piece of music.

violin: A four-stringed instrument. Its clear tone and versatility has made it one of the most popular of all western orchestral instruments.

vocal cords: The ribbons of skin which stretch across the larynx in the throat and vibrate as you talk or sing. The vocal cords are the strings of your own musical instrument — your voice.

zither: A stringed instrument found in many parts of the world. There are several kinds: tube zithers are small enough to hold in the hand and long zithers are usually rested on a surface to be played.

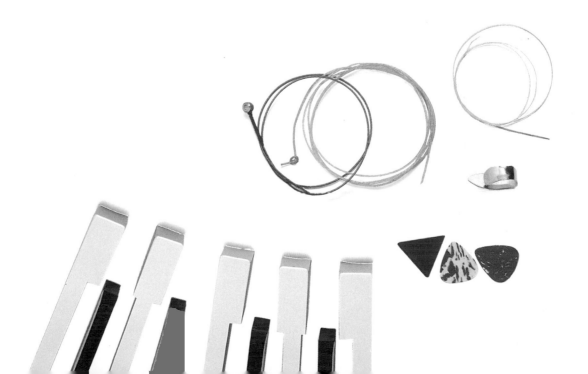

INDEX

A
Africa   6, 7, 28
alto   12, 37
amplifier   22
Ancient Greece   14
Apache Indian   8–9
Asia   4, 6, 8, 17, 26–27, 29
Austria   33, 37, 41

B
Bach, Johann Sebastian   31, 38
banjo   18–19
bass   12, 37
bass bar   10
bass clef   24
baton   34–35
Beatles, The   27, 39
bottleneck   21
bow   6, 8, 10–11
bridge   9, 10, 28

C
cantata   38
Caravaggio, Michelangelo Merisi da   16
cello   12–13
chin rest   10
China   4, 17, 28
choir   38–39
choral music   38–39
chord   25
Chung, Kyung Wah   11
classical guitar   20–21
clavichord   30
conductor   34–35
consort   10
counter tenor   37
Cristofori, Bartolomeo   31
crossbar   14–15
crotchet   25

D
damper   32
dancing   9, 20, 41
double bass   5, 12–13
drone string   26
dulcimer   29

E
electric guitar   22–23
England   11, 19, 27, 39

Ethiopia   15

F
Fabris, Pietro   9
Fender, Leo   22
fingerboard   8, 10, 16, 19, 20
folk fiddle   8–9
Formby, George   19
fret   16–17, 26

G
Germany   31, 38, 40–41
Gibson, Orville   22
gospel music   39
guitar   20–23
Gypsy Kings, The   21

H
harp   15
harpsichord   31
Hendrix, Jimi   23
Hungary   32

I
improvisation   25, 26
India   25, 26–27
Italy   9, 11, 16, 40, 41

J
Japan   6, 25, 28
jazz   13, 23, 39

K
keyboard instruments   30–33
Korea   11, 29
koto   28–29

L
larynx   36
Liszt, Franz   32
loudspeaker   22
lute   16–17
lyre   14–15

M
Menuhin, Yehudi   11, 27
metronome   42
microphone   37
Mingus, Charlie   13
minim   25
Monteverdi, Claudio   40

moon guitar   17
Mozart, Wolfgang Amadeus   33, 41
muezzin   37
multiple string bow   7
musical bow   6-7
musical   41

N
New Zealand   40–41
note   5, 8, 9, 13, 15, 16, 17, 24–25, 29, 30–31,
    32–33, 34, 36, 42–43

O
octave   25
opera   40–41
oratorio   38
orchestra   10, 34–35
Orpheus   14

P
Paganini, Niccolò   11
Paul, Les   23
pedals   23, 31
pegs   9, 10
pentatonic scale   25
Peru   15
piano   31, 32–33
pitch   8, 29, 43
plectrum   19, 21, 31
plucking   4–5, 6, 18–19
Portugal   17
Puccini, Giacomo   41

Q
quaver   25

R
raga   26
resin   10–11
resonator   5, 7, 10, 13, 15, 16, 20, 32, 36
rock and roll   23, 27, 38

S
scale   25, 26, 36
Segovia, Andrés   20
semibreve   24
Shankar, Ravi   27
short-necked fiddle   8–9
singing   36–41
sitar   26–27

soprano   36
soundboard   32
soundhole   11, 21
soundpost   11
South America   21
Spain   20–21
spike fiddle   8–9
staves   24
Stradivari, Antonio   11
string quartet   12
string quintet   12–13
sympathetic string   26

T
tabla   27
Tarantella with Posillipo in the Background   9
Te Kanawa, Kiri   40–41
tenor   12–13, 36
Tibet   29
Torres, Antonio   20
treble   12, 36
treble clef   24
tuning   5, 34, 43
tuning fork   43
Turandot   41
Turkey   8

U
ukulele   18–19
United States of America   9, 13, 18, 23, 39

V
vibration   4, 5, 6, 8, 11, 16, 22, 23, 26, 29, 30, 32,
    36, 43
viol   10
viola   13
violin   10–12
vocal cords   36–37
voice   36–41

W
Wagner, Richard   40

Y
yodelling   37
Young Man Playing a Lute   16

Z
zither   28–29

IMP Academy Manuscript

ACKNOWLEDGEMENTS

The publishers would like to thank the following for permission to reproduce these photographs:

Ace Photo Agency for string quintet (page 12). Clive Barda Performing Arts Library for Khung Wha Chung (page 11); orchestra (page 34/35); choir (page 38); Lucia Popp (page 40); scene from *Turandot* (pages 40/41) and musical programme (page 41). Bridgeman Art Library for Paganini (page 11); *Young Man Playing a Lute* by Caravaggio (page 16) and harpsichord (page 31). E.T. Archive for *Tarantella With Posillipo in Background* by Pietro Fabris. The Horniman Museum and Gardens for lyre (page 15) and Portugese fish lute (page 17). Hutchison Library for Chinese string band (page 4); musical bow from Hitacas (page 7); Peruvian harp player (page 15); Chinese moon guitar player (page 17); Indian print of a sitar player (page 26); Tibetan village orchestra (page 29) and South Korean Koto player (page 29). Redferns for Charlie Mingus (page 13); The Gypsy Kings (page 21); Jimi Hendrix (page 23); Ravi Shankar (page 27) and gospel choir (page 39). Sefton Photo Library for Andrés Segovia (page 20). Colonial Williamsburg Foundation, Virginia, for American painting from the 1800s (page 18).

The publishers would also like to give special thanks to Carole Mahoney and Danny Staples for their original synopsis, to Mickleburgh Music Shop, Bristol for the loan of musical instruments and to David Stannard for his help with photography.